IN TAKING APART A KALEIDOSCOPE

In Taking Apart a Kaleidoscope

POEMS

ADAM ZHOU

© 2019 Adam Zhou

Cover art: Keitma

book design: adam b. bohannon

Book editors: Michael Broder and Samantha Pious

Published by Indolent Books,

an imprint of Indolent Arts Foundation, Inc.

indolentbooks.com

Brooklyn, New York

ISBN: 978-1-945023-24-8

Special thanks to Epic Sponsor Megan Chinburg for helping to fund the production of this book.

CONTENTS

Nomenclature 3

Flight 4

How to Build a Desert 5

In Taking Apart a Kaleidoscope 6

Anti-Confessions 7

Haikai No Ku 8

Reverse Oneirology 9

The 3 Stages Before a Farewell 11

my mother 12

the woman next door 13

a sonnet for plastic chairs 14

Ripple Effect 15

home, 1945 17

A Displacement of Time Which Is Not a Displacement of Time but a Displacement of Space 19

Elegy for a Dying Animal 20

witness statement to the national police 21

By Morning 22

Stale Goods 23

Semi-Objectivism 24

Cause Célèbre 25

Post-Funeral Ruminations 26

Conflicting Images 28

Dictations of the Great Mao 29

A Journey, Trailed 30

Slices of Spring 31

Undulations 33

View from the NOAA Okeanos Explorer 34

Cloaked 35

A Beginner's Guide to the Chinese Language 36

Inverse 38

the roman maidens 39

Art Theft 40

woven light 41

Contemporary Origami 43

Symphony No. 2, Resurrection 44

NOTES 45

ACKNOWLEDGMENTS 47

ABOUT THE AUTHOR 49

ABOUT INDOLENT BOOKS 50

IN TAKING APART A KALEIDOSCOPE

Nomenclature

People call him by his mother's name:
    凤, which means phoenix, or in another context,

wind. Are they not the same thing,
    just one without its *cheongsam*?

He wants to remember
    how to turn off the darkness, feel the sunlight

envelop him like the walls
    of a mother's womb. He knows that soon

the gates will tear apart. For now,
    he will shake away his feathers. For now,

he will let wings swallow wings
    so that all that's left are the speckles

of ashes. He'll want to feed them
    the imagery and the lyrics of a Tang poet

hoping that in their flight, 凤
    can also mean the ink on a parchment

seeping into a new poem.

flight

after dinner, the landscape will remain stubborn,
still dressed in a sullen light. incense: cut grass
and yearning running amidst the green-gray sea of the mountains.

their trees march alongside us; this is the secret
that won't show in the *malas* of memories. a reflection in the river.
a reflection that steps off into the stars, melting

drops to a solitary daffodil. its petals outstretched, crying out
for the warmth of light a moon cannot give. a silent echo.
you'll pick it up and hear a snap, a wave

of goodbye. it will travel with us with gasping breath,
imitating our own. a door, waiting, welcoming
us with the absence of green and blue like it's saying

patches of gray won't well their tears into the scars
we have etched into concrete ground. a white skull
laughs, ready to fly without a body.

How to Build a Desert

1.
I imagine you snuggled into the arms of a fog. Something that doesn't grow like the city, five-thirty in the afternoon. If I were there, we'd watch the birds revolve around our shadows. Counting the seconds until a foehn wind tips over some of the leaves from the mahogany trees above, we'd be flushed and warm. Oh, wait for me like you'd wait for the sunset.

2.
They'd enter as animals from the home across the brook. Paws and hooves fluttering across dry land. Eyeing pityingly, I think you disappoint them, for you are not perfection, merely an illusion thereof. The morning darkens as they leave, but promise you'll step into whiteness over by the fields. There's something new if your heart hasn't stopped.

3.
Since you left, the sea slid back, hiding crackling waves of blue. It sits contemplating the world, whispering to me something inaudible. Maybe it wants to know the dusted dreams of the grass blades or the artist's palette of the blurred sun. I'll not speak. All I will do is break my shell. Let me watch the shards scatter across the limestone shore.

In Taking Apart a Kaleidoscope

A little boy, dressed in his father's clothes.
The fragments of a lullaby. A blend
of musical notes. Of chords that shape
adventures. Shapes hang above a cot
and hide away. One of them,
a soul. A soul isn't meant to feel
like fabric. Something to tear.
Something to outgrow. Footsteps,
cautious. A metronome to this prelude.
Eyes wander over windows. And doors.
And mirrors. Any presence of an entrance.
Locks prefer not to accept keys.

Anti-Confessions

While you were away,
   I could **hear** the tapping noise
every time the sky
   painted itself in dark
colors. Mother always says
   list **the** possibilities
but no: doors and windows
   bolted. The same way
the **flowers** in the backyard
   fold in their layers and depths
from the trance of night.
   Remember the ghost stories?
How you saw the silver wisps rise
   and linger over our beds?
Cower at pages yellowing
   at the corners, but as for me,
I choose to **celebrate**. Cold wind,
   cold stars. I almost feel them
swirl around me as if this were a dance
   and I let my steps trace the beat
before the weight of gravity
   makes it **burn**. This is me
breathing. Living is all about the descent.
Hear the flowers celebrate and burn.

Haikai No Ku

I was satisfied
with the way you danced the waltz
until your fingers

mimicked beating drums.
A cadence gathering speed.
Staccatos drowning

and yet breathing more
than ever. They make me see
the bruises under

my clothes. I used glue
to patch sequins and stained glass
and flowers and flesh.

I feel your fingers
now gripping, peeling off scraps
to keep for yourself

but beware. My eyes
once touched can never be healed.
So, come. Come closer.

Reverse Oneirology

my brother wakes me up
by splitting apart my eyes.
behind them, there's a river
for his gaze to drift in.
                      the next time
             he enters my bedroom
        he'll tell me he's a monster
                          inside.
a fake in my reveries:
an adolescent cries
because he thinks
he hears sounds
under the bed.
they demand
the white
flags.
              lullabies—thunderous
              in the background
              and no one to tell me why
              i still hear footsteps
                    coming closer.
my heart
is smothered in droplets
of water. tears,
which are poison. i savor it.
                      lately,
                I've been running

under the underbelly
of the sky—rendered transparent. it's hard
to tell the difference between shadows and ghosts.

The 3 Stages Before a Farewell

1.
To remember what rawness feels like
I give my soul to the long-lost uncle
but he wanted my flesh. How easy it is
to cut away the blemishes with a knife.

2.
My voice. A wounded pig. My fingers
wrapped around the necks of newborns
telling them no one hears anything I say.

3.
I write a farewell letter on bedroom walls.
I feel the cracks that surround the words—
they are cold. I can almost hear the sound
inside them swallowing. I want to laugh.

my mother

explained to me that even if she loved me
she could forget my name and so i think
i can still love her. sorry. i have to watch
pictures crumple and surrender in her arms
as if it were my heart, warm, pulsing.
light, blank. maybe that's how i feel.

i see a tree and a boy and a dog and a sun and a man and a car
and a cloud and a cross.

the woman next door

a chinese woman lives next door, and i hear her whispers when i head to bed, words like *beautiful* repeated without end as if putting them together would stir up an entirely different meaning. maybe something like emptiness, something quivering in the arms of a fog. i've seen her gaze so many times, a palette of misty amber that trickles down into its reflection; sliced-up memories in the desert of a stomach. sometimes i feel the shadow of her eyes tailgating that of mine, making sure to send trickles of sand into my path. cluster adds onto cluster, yet i don't know what to see. tomorrow, i'll ask for her guidance, before shaking her gloved hands and whispering *bye auntie mei.*

a sonnet for plastic chairs

in the light of the morning's rays shining
on the porch, it's just the four of us, you,
me, mom, and dad, sitting on those plastic
chairs auntie would never let us buy just
because they were too ugly, but now she's
dead and all we're doing is drinking chai,
careful not to spill it on our black suits
and even blacker feelings—yes, it's true
we still meet every thursday to whisper
sounds of solace, but no, we aren't sad
or else auntie's shadow will seep into
gusts of wind and reprimand us with cruel
blows—now it's evening, and when you leave, we
head inside, watching ourselves disappear

Ripple Effect

For the little boy who shattered the porcelain pot and didn't
    pick up the pieces
recite after me
沉默 doesn't mean the same thing in China.
Not the absence of sound.
Only the weight of melancholy.
Each sliver that pierces
the concrete floor
echoes and still there is 沉默.

Back when I didn't know *Yeye*
except for his silhouette on the porch
unmoving in the rocking chair
basking in the moon's embrace
he would murmur words
I could not understand not because I couldn't hear them
but because I did not know the language:
the only thread that could have brought us together.
Only later as my mother let the light filter through the stars
did I realize he was talking about the porcelain pot.

He brought it back from the carnage of the Cultural
    Revolution
and though all the color had paled
to a dull copper flame adorned with nothing but scars
(much like himself)

it was the only way to block the weight of melancholy
from taking over as long as the lid stayed on.

Tonight, there will be no hand to guide him
from the pagodas, their walls crumbling from the bullets.
No lamplight to cast shadows
on the blood-stained puddles
or the bodies too cold
to move, to be whisped away
into vapor.

home, 1945

little boy whistling
daddy's army songs.

just air to stop him.
his lips warm, his tune

not. as the morning
breaks open cities

watch them bloom flowers:
their petals smothered

in flames and remnants
of tattered skin. skies

always swallow prey
into their bunkers

and so will the night
be just as lovely?

sometimes, it is best
to keep on walking

alone. without hands
to hold, footsteps lead

to the dead center
of nowhere—

au fond, of everything else.
the clouds, the dirt roads,

the boyish nightmares.

A Displacement of Time Which Is Not a Displacement of Time but a Displacement of Space

We are standing in the middle of the street
    holding hands, watching
flies dance around our bodies.
    Raindrops start following us
disguising themselves as mirrors
    so that we can see all the people
who tell us to break ourselves.
    We are holding hands
feeling our skin burning at the touch.
    How painful it is
to feel alive in the first few minutes
    of death. To imagine
what it must be like to let fingers
    slip out of one's grasp
and find, in their place, the leftover shards
    of a crystal ball.
After a few years, people will stand here
    in the middle of the street,
not hurting, never knowing the nights that passed before them.

Elegy for a Dying Animal

There was a crippled dog
sitting beside my feet. Gray feathers, crumpled, limp.
Gray flesh already floating
within lost days.
I think about how when I look down
all I see are the leftovers
of what we call machines
pregnant with ammunition—these orbs
wondrous
in the way they can make
a disappearance
sound like an arpeggio,
feel like a fire pushed onto lips.
Later I will sleep
ignoring the fact that water
finally can leak
into pillows
because the *accelerando*, the *da capo de la danse* is yet to come.
Thinking of something else now.
The silent plea
of a dying animal:
this can't be real.

witness statement to the national police

i read
about how beggars
come running to the theatre
for the weekend features.
last time,
a boy
ate sixteen bullets.
the finale:
shadows
intertwining
with the spilled
liquid.

seconds pass
and i'm the only stranger
who is left here.
i'm still waiting
for the applause.
the closing
of the curtains.
what else
but to pretend
i've lost
the key
to my house.

By Morning

Your hands caress
walls caked in blood
from a wounded face
even the drapes can't hide.
The intimacy is bothersome.
There will be no tomb for the body
and so the flesh will continue to strip
away. Catch the flaring pieces
as they draw stains
on your skin. A palette
of raw crimson. The paints wrinkling.
Admire the craft, while still knowing
that the true treasure lies underneath.
A butcher,
and in his hands, a blade.

Stale Goods

Ten years should pass
       for one to adjust to the darkness
                      of unblinking eyes
and even if a man
       were to stare at the irides
               a small pair of mirrors
he would discover
       not his reflection
              but a yawning hole spilling
back into the river
       now as clear as the water
                now as rippled as the scars
       of a body whose hands
             never offered
                   pink carnations.

Semi-Objectivism

He is not sure about waking

        outside the graveyard

to find his body split

        open like snow peeling

in the face of a sunrise

        like a flower blooming

in reverse. When it's dark

        he will wander into homes

listening for the sound

        of a train. No. Whispers.

He thinks his parents

        are inside the funnel

waiting for the right

        time to take shape as smoke

so at last their destination

        will be able to surround

stone crosses forever.

        Home sweet home. Departure

comes in many forms

        but if only he could see them.

Cause Célèbre

Children left naked in ponds, unattended.

Even when drunk, black water leaves no shadows.

A cloth, a layer of skin, some threads sticking out.

Only fish can taste their flesh: sweet and raw.

Chests rise and collapse almost simultaneously.

Spry laughter, a dissonance caught in a loop.

Post-Funeral Ruminations

I'll drink from my glass
the same way a red apple
drops onto the ground:
the sound should be deafening.

Ripples.

As I run in circles, I start to freeze.
Ink-stained footprints scatter
to find a place of arrival
and yet everywhere looks the same
because people turn away
from their own shadow.

Not me. My unlicked body
is bound to a ring.
It seethes in its frame
like a pendulum. My drink
too, seethes, flutters in the tightness
of my mouth.
I am deep enough to drown.
I cannot remember how I heard the glass break.
Cannot remember when or how.

I'll collect the jagged pieces.
Put them in a plastic bag.
Trick myself into thinking
that these too won't melt
and slip between my fingers.

Conflicting Images

As for sunsets, dying goddesses,
whatever they're called now,
they're alone again. Bodies
collapse and watch tragedies
without endings. They stare
at raw slivers of light, thinking
that its blood paints itself
in flamboyant colors to hide
pain. Deities collect hearts
the same way rays disperse
on windowsills, but that's only
in fiction. In real life,
they prepare to build graves,
letting each fistful of dirt
weave through their fingers
before reaching its target.
Every night, they make sure
that their magnum opus,
basking in newfound color,
is near done, but not too near.

Dictations of the Great Mao

look deep inside the eyes
of the people who taught us
to bury the dead. you will see
a small clutch of plum blossoms
open like a fist. ground them. soak
them in water. pour this tea
for your *nai nai*. let it spill
across the table
down to her feet. you will drink
once the skin stops burning.
no cups. only hands marbled
with the blood of our flag.
nai nai will collect the leftovers
in spoons, so bless each drop
with holy water, recite lines
from the treasured red book:
it's always darkest before 日 出
but morning never came
for her. mourning did,
walking over the war-torn
rice fields with a leaky umbrella,
yet this time, the fluid
will have already shred itself
into the shards of a hammer and sickle.

A Journey, Trailed
After Du Fu

Every week, I come by to see pale leaves
settle on wet ground, breathing through their stems

songs on the dance of the jasmine flowers,
painted with the shimmering moon's white light.

I see their shadows rippling on the skin
of a lake as if it were frost and snow,

even if the light behind my eyes fades
into the landscape of a parallel dream.

I fold it onto itself, persuading
memories of a wandering pilgrim

to dissipate once more onto bare ground.
I peel its remnants. A scent like mud.

It follows me to the pagodas of Henan,
and when candles are lit

they illuminate nothing.

Slices of Spring

The trickle of the nearby
stream—a faint whisper
of a rusty flute,

gentle in the way
it would move
from ear to

ear of a wandering traveler
before the diluting
sound sent him

on his way. So, plant yourself
in the troupe of Pan's
company, where emerald

leaves and golden rays
trickle down onto soft
ground. Listen once more,

maybe a falling plum
from a good tree will
bring reward for your toils

and the chatter of jays
mask envy that
calls the scrutiny

of a nearby stream whose
détaché prayer
surges, and reaches its

zenith. Hurried footsteps crackle
over a blanket of dry leaves,
though each landing is gentle,
as soft as cat-steps.

Undulations

A wave takes shape in the form
of a human body, shrouded in a fiery dress
as if making sure scattered footprints
can at last find, in its mind's cranny, a faint glint.
Like a passage stretching out

coarse fingers onto a child's body.
Perhaps it may find eyes hiding behind
the hours of night. The coarse landscape
you do not seem to know because feeble tears
etch red marks on skin. They never fade,

so let the wave wash against a shadow. Let its body,
vacant and wandering, take shape
as a raft, drowned by its own planks,
as if making sure scattered bones, not fully grown,
can at last find, on the ocean floor, a home.

View from the *NOAA Okeanos Explorer*

Wait until the fluctuations of life
reflect upon the skin of the waves
dressed in a gown of sapphires
and glittered gold by a rising sun
so at last you can hear the songs
of a mother trickling out of the cavities
in the ocean floor and even if the words
are hushed every syllable clings on
like air before sliding splashing
sinking back to where it came from

The solitary moon seems to give no light
to the marbled surface of the water tinted
with a black that once belonged only to night
but let the shadows of a collage patched
together with wrinkled waste trickle out
of the darkness and swallow up what is left

Cloaked

today, we'll see the cloak of death
removed from the ocean's shoulders
but still wisps of black strands remain
hidden in every trough of the waves

choosing to take shape as
crumpled plastic bags soaked dark
with the gore of strangled sea turtles.
you can see this exhibit while crouching

over sand and shells that mingle with the grains
of broken wine glasses and candy wrappers.
they take sail into the deep waters, knowing
that this is the one landscape without an exit.

only rancor will settle here like a baby bird
and it will tell us to swim away. we swim
and we do it without stopping to picture
what might happen if we made another choice.

A Beginner's Guide to the Chinese Language

1.
Copy the old man
scratching the calligraphy
into his palm with his dirt caked fingernails.
He writes 福 upside down
the way all the Chinese neighbors
place their lucky posters on the front door.

2.
Once the skin starts to turn red
think to yourself that red means
joy and prosperity and fortune
and beauty and power. Not pain.

3.
The cadence of the word rolling on your tongue
should make you conscious
of the winding movements it makes. Four
different tones form an uncomposed song
that scatters into different paths.
Make sure the *glissando* does not strangle
itself upon the mocking laughter
of those who do not speak the language.

4.
Let others start to wrap the chains
around your throat. They think
they will force out the gaunt accent.
Question if they do not see
the scarlet scales forming
into a *shenlong* dragon, one that spindles
through the lantern-filled sky
with a tune so furiously blooming.

Inverse

        Hands can't cup
images painted over waves.
                Petals of sun,
           streams of chrysanthemum.
      How quickly they trickle
           through my fingers.

Now, an image
        I care for. A face:
                eyes, nose, lips
and knowing the skin
        is glass,
           already shattered.

the roman maidens

look outside, and you'll find yourself floating
between the negative space that you call
darkness
    something that you see dressed in robes,
    chanting to guide you here, because your
    spirit
        still spies on some shapeless sight,
        dancing under the strewn pieces of
        cloud
            or maybe it's smoke and smog,
            a palette that speaks to you in a
            veil
                as if the roman maidens
                are at last releasing the firm
                grasp
                    of chains and as the hunting dogs
                    look up at the doves, they too will
                    find themselves floating in darkness

Art Theft

I like to paint / over a painting / just to see / if the story it tells / the one with the purple sky / and below it / a pair of silhouettes / changes into one / I'm actually in. / It's fine if I'm stood / behind the trunks of the autumn trees / or in the form of a lone sparrow / or even hidden in the crevices of the minds of two children. There's a bottle of tears / under my bed / and as I let the substance spill / onto my fingers / and slither / into the nooks of the frame / I watch a blue-gray sea / of scattered memories / ripple against its own waves. / The landscape / now is darkness. / Perhaps there was nothing / to begin with / and so I'll start / my own journey. / The brushes / on blank canvas / pave a never ending / road.

woven light

flirting in the closet. stop. someone pulling away threads—

advertisements for museums,   closed,
        but not locked.
it's a window.   untitled, 1992. oil on canvas?
    no, just a reflection.

—painting them in ochre colors—

        the son of man has only moved itself
    further into pollock's   panorama.
    the persistence of memory
trapped within la grande jatte's flood water

—and still the canvas is something to be felt, not looked at—

    expressionism wrinkles
    itself within the human experience.
        if only the dynamism of it all
unfurled   itself to the streets outside.

—or maybe the lisping voices from behind—

            imagine hands smothered
over a parallel universe.   hiding.
        they clasp onto the melted pigments,
still seeing the dawn,   the borrowed body.

—will reveal the self-sacrifice. a rhythm so fluidly perpetual.

Contemporary Origami

My reach does not stop
  at the wings of a crane.
It stretches out to a field

  empty. Boy, listen
to me, I am above the soil
  I am flying. Thrown.

There's something lovely
  about how things hide
away. A fold onto itself

  still cannot portray
creases like knives, no
  blood. Easy to trace.

Easy to have my hands
  hold one thousand
cranes in the flesh.

  Make them dance.
Feel the wrinkled feathers.
  Hear the sound of bones
disguise into a cadenza.

Symphony No. 2, Resurrection

Yes, they left town when the small bird wept.
Some say it mimicked the songs their mama adored.
Others say it's the papa, or one of the two daughters
but they all sleep blanketed under soil. The patch
in the backyard. Every strand of grass
grows out of the pores of crisp, darkened skin.
Every strand curls into a treble clef, and later
the sharps, the flats, the hurried turn of notes.

For melodies like to rise and say
there isn't room to land.
They like to fly and dress
in a pair of wings.

NOTES

"Nomenclature," page 3:
The Chinese ideograph 凤 (pinyin: fènghuáng), English fenghuang, refers to a bird of East Asian mythology identified with the phoenix of Western mythology. *The cheongsam*, literally "long gown," is a traditional type of tight-fitting Chinese women's dress.

"Flight," page 4:
The *mala* is a string of prayer beads used in Buddhism and other Eastern religious and spiritual traditions to focus attention while repeating a mantra or the name of a divine being.

"*Haikai No Ku*," page 8:
The term *haikai no ku* (Japanese) refers to a verse of *haikai*, a popular genre of Japanese linked verse developed in the sixteenth century.

"Ripple Effect," page 15:
The Chinese ideograph 沉默 (pinyin: chénmò) represents the Chinese word for "silence." In Mandarin, *yeye* is the most commonly used word for a paternal grandfather.

"Dictations of the Great Mao," page 29:
In Mandarin, *nai nai* is the most commonly used word for a paternal grandmother. The Chinese ideograph 日出 (pinyin: rì chū) represent the Chinese word for "sunrise."

"A Beginner's Guide to the Chinese Language," page 36:
The Chinese ideograph 福 (pinyin: Fú) represents the Chinese character *Fú*, meaning "fortune" or "good luck." The Chinese word *shenlong* refers to a dragon of Chinese mythology.

ACKNOWLEDGMENTS

These poems originally appeared, sometimes in different versions or with different titles, in the following publications.

Alexandria Quarterly: "Post-Funeral Ruminations"
Blue Marble Review: "Art Theft"
Bridge: The Bluffton University Literary Journal: "woven light"
Eunoia Review: "By Morning," "Haikai No Ku," "Anti-Confessions"
di-vêrsé-city Youth Anthology 2018: "A Displacement of Time Which Is Not a Displacement of Time but a Displacement of Space"
Glass: A Journal of Poetry: "Reverse Oneirology"
Hyphen: "A Beginner's Guide to the Chinese Language"
K'in: "Dictations of the Great Mao," "Nomenclature"
The Kill List Chronicles: "witness statement to the national police"
Lunch Ticket: "Four from the Graveyard"
Polyphony Lit: "Dictations of the Great Mao"
Quail Bell Magazine: "the roman maidens"
The Rising Phoenix Review: "Contemporary Origami"
What Rough Beast: "*Cause Célèbre*," "Undulations," "Inverse," "Stale Goods," "the woman next door"

For my fellow storytellers:
Scott Platt-Salcedo, who has guided me since the very beginning of my writing journey; Mama, Baba, and Mandy, for the childhood stories which have always stuck with me;

Michael Heiss, Mary Kate Turner, Vivian Zhao, Yulian Ye, Prachi Kondapuram, Bryan Dong, Hansol Choi, Charith Reddy, Jessica Vu, Hannah Ahn, Megan Li, Alison Chan, Diana Zhao, and William Feng from the Creative Nonfiction Course at CTY 16, for helping me see words in a different light; Carly Joy Miller, Peter LaBerge, and Matthew Gellman from the Adroit Mentorship Program Class of 2017, for being such amazing role models; Katrina Baker, for her kind, thoughtful mentorship; Robert Butcher and Nicole Gough for instilling my love of literature; Woosuk Kim, Minsoo Kang, and Martin Jee with *The McKinley Review*; and Michael Broder and Bob Carr, for believing in me and making everything possible.

ABOUT THE AUTHOR

Adam Zhou, a Chinese national, was born and raised in the Philippines. He has honed his poetry craft with support from programs including the Center for Talented Youth, the Adroit Mentorship Program, and the University of Iowa Young Writers' Studio Online. Zhou has been recognized by the Scholastic Art and Writing Awards at the national level, and his work has appeared in *The Rising Phoenix Review, Blue Marble Review, Glass: A Journal of Poetry, Lunch Ticket*, and other journals. Zhou is a winner of the Norman Maclean Nonfiction Award from Aerie International, a literary journal featuring work by high school youth worldwide, produced by the students of Big Sky High School in Missoula, Montana. He won the Kathy Carlson and Emily Stauffer Award from *Apogee*, and was one of ten Asian American high school writers included in *Hyphen* magazine's Youth Poetry Folio for National Poetry Month in 2019. Zhou is the founding editor of *The McKinley Review*, a literary journal based in the international community of the Philippines and focusing on the natural environment. His research papers on the socioecological system of the Cordillera Rice Terraces have been presented at conferences and published in journals internationally. When this collection was published, Zhou was a high school senior at the International School Manila.

ABOUT INDOLENT BOOKS

Founded in 2015, Indolent Books is a nonprofit poetry press based in Brooklyn, with staff working remotely around the country. In our books and on our website, Indolent publishes work by poets and writers who are queer, trans, nonbinary (or gender nonconforming), intersex, women, people of color, people living with HIV, people with histories of addiction, abuse, and other traumatic experiences, and other poets and writers who are underrepresented or marginalized, or whose work has particular relevance to issues of racial, social, economic, and environmental justice. We also focus on poets over 50 without a first book. Indolent is committed to an inclusive workplace. Indolent Books is an imprint of Indolent Arts, a 501(c)(3) charity.

www.ingramcontent.com/pod-product-compliance
Lightning Source LLC
Chambersburg PA
CBHW030134100526
44591CB00009B/652